Thanks to My Parents

American President
Volunteers Award 2023
Irvine, CA

Youth Self-Development Seminar
Temple City, CA, 10/2023

YSDC Seminar
Yorba Linda, CA, 1/2024

Youth Self-Development Seminar
Irvine, CA, 10/2023

We like YSDC uniform

Thanks Giving Activity
Yorba Linda B, CA 2023

Youth Effectiveness Trai
Irvine, CA, 20

漫谈心青少年自我成长俱乐部
感恩节聚会
11/2022，Irvine,CA

Y.E.T. Workshop
Irvine CA 2023

WHAT MAKES YOU HAPPY?

The Wisdom from Psychologists and Youths

Jeson Zhang

HAT MAKES YOU HAPPY?

e Wisdom from Psychologists and Youths

Table of Contents

FOREWORD (English Version)

The Origin

People often ask me curiously, "Why did you study psychology in the first place? Were you depressed?"

Now that I think about the opportunity to embark on the path of self-growth, I am not depressed, but it is also because I am unhappy. I was living in China then, living in a decent house, having a decent car, owning a decent career, and having a decent husband and children, but I was still unhappy; what was wrong?

Later, I went to see a psychological counselor once or twice. After the counseling, I felt the world was beautiful and that there was nothing wrong with the outside. If I had to find a mistake, it would be that my vision of the world from the heart was "wrong." The most significant benefit of counseling sessions for me is not only that I have regained my happiness but also that I have discovered another wonderful world—it turns out that in addition to the external material world of fame and fortune, there is also an inner world, where all my joys and sorrows come to fruition.

From here, I began to embark on a path of self-development, happiness, and my life mission. I took many psychology courses and entered the field of psychoeducation.

The Discovery

I came to the U.S. in 2015, which is at the forefront of psychological science and inner growth. I've found that many first-generation immigrants, whether they've just arrived in the U.S. or even old immigrants who have been in the U.S. for decades, still have very different ideologies from Americans. Perhaps it was the cultural background difference from the roots of living in China when they were children, or it was difficult to deeply integrate into American society after coming to the United States because of language and cultural issues, so the cutting-edge psychological science and inner growth resources of the United States were not applied and absorbed more effectively by too many Chinese immigrants.

This shows two interesting phenomena:

1. Many Chinese immigrants in the United States are still busy with the most basic survival and security needs of human nature, and it is difficult to pursue higher-level inner growth and self-realization needs. Of course, this phenomenon has no superiority or inferiority, just different states of life.

(Thanks to the author, Jeson, for elaborating on the humanistic theory of intrinsic needs in more detail in the following chapters, which would help you understand these paragraphs much more clearly);

2. A small number of people need to self-grow. Still, because of language barriers and different cultures, it is difficult for them to effectively use the abundant and leading scientific and environmental resources of the United States.

I think I have a specific professional accumulation in psychology; I have worked as an English teacher at a Chinese university and have a foundation in English. I have been practicing self-development and have a lot of experience and lessons, all of which can contribute to my dream - I hope to become a bridge between China and the United States, build a road of communication between psychological science and inner growth, and help more Chinese people live happily.

Because, whether in the United States or China, whether it is a working person or a stay-at-home wife, isn't happiness what everyone wants in the end?

The Dream

Based on my dream, I have continued to learn and obtain many certificates in parenting, intimacy, and personal growth in my nearly ten years in America. I founded AMDREO, a non-profit organization; I conduct group and one-on-one classes and tutoring for adults and teenagers. I spread the positive American curriculum I have learned to Chinese people in America. I hope to help more and more people live happier lives with scientific methods. I want to thank my husband for his moral and material support so that I can do what I love.

The main curriculum system I am currently leading is a series of interpersonal relationship courses developed by American psychologist Dr. Thomas Gordon, including "Parent Effectiveness Training," "Youth Effectiveness Training," and "Teacher Effectiveness Training. " I am also about to launch the "Leadership Effectiveness Training" workshops. At the same time, I also lead groups or one-on-one on topics such as intimacy and emotional management.

At the same time, my son, Jeson Zhang, also the author of this book, launched the Youth Self-Development Club (Y.S.D.C.) in 2022 to lead more youths to learn and apply these scientific concepts and tools. As a result, AMDREO has been awarded the official certification organization of the U.S. Presidential Volunteer Award.

Youth public welfare seminars are held every weekend in several cities in the Los Angeles area, and teenagers discuss self-development. This book includes seminar reports on the theme of "The

4

Gifts from Life" and testimonials from young leaders of Y.S.D.C. who received the 2023 President's Volunteer Award.

My Happiness

Many people are puzzled, saying, "Mandy, you work so hard for sharing and don't make much money. Why?"

Many praise it, saying, "Mandy, you have great love. You don't care about your gains and losses."

I like the theory of humanistic psychologist Dr. Gordon: One's behavior only because it satisfies one's inner needs. This simple theory has helped me see many truths.

So, I do these things not because I'm stupid or noble but because they satisfy my inner needs – talking about inner growth with like-minded participants and fulfilling my need for social and emotional communication. More people are happier because of my help, which satisfies my need for accomplishment. Leading and supporting others allowed me to experience a steady stream of creativity and vitality and meet the needs for self-realization. Learning, practicing, and sharing have allowed me to experience more and more of the richness and excitement of my inner world; they also helped me to understand more and more of my true self and others, which has made me always walk on the road of happiness back to my nature...

Therefore, happiness is straightforward: knowing the heart, satisfying inner needs, being responsible for oneself, and helping others simultaneously.

I can be the master of my happiness, and so can you.

The Gifts

Here, I would like to give a special thanks to the author of this book, my son, Jeson Zhang. He is the angel who reaps this gift of happiness in my life.

First, I thank Jeson for being a valuable testing ground for me.

As an instructor who leads parenting and youth classes, it isn't easy to be convincing if I have not practiced in-depth or don't have much experience supporting teenagers' growth. Jeson is an important testing ground and growth base for me. In him, the effects of every skill used and the insight from every practice all helped me build up my teaching ability constantly; even though I have a lot of in-depth contact with teenagers in youth groups or one-on-one classes, it is not comparable to the seamless enhancement that Jeson has brought me. In him, I see the effects of a humanistic approach to parenting, which makes my work even more motivating.

Second, I thank Jeson for being my teacher assistant.

Jeson ultimately made up for the lack of English as my second language and the inevitable generation gap between the young students and me. He also added too much to the liveliness and integration of the course, making our courses even more engaging. At the same time, he is also my mentor; he works with me to produce course materials, gives me feedback on the effectiveness of the course, and discusses various cases and topics about parents, teenagers, and even human development. I often ask him about teenagers' perspectives. In addition, his mastery of the course content and outstanding practice have made me more confident in the course and my teaching. What makes me even more gratifying is that the AMDREO Youth Self-Development Club he founded not only created a practice of his self-growth but also helped more peers grow together and even made my life mission of helping myself and others continue.

Third, I thank Jeson for being my child. My husband and I grew up in China, and Jeson grew up in the United States; there was a big difference between us: he couldn't understand our idioms, and we couldn't understand his jokes. The stars he likes, the games he plays, the music he listens to, the books he reads, etc., are basically blind spots for us. The education and social philosophy of the United States are very different from that of China. As his parents, we also have a lot of expectations for him. Therefore, when there is such a big difference in language and culture, and adolescence meets menopause, we have many values collisions; we also often have arguments and occasionally yell at each other. Still, fortunately, our whole family has been learning together and using scientific and effective methods so that our relationship bank is always full of balance. As Dr. Gordon said, parents are human beings, not gods; reality is more important than perfection. I also often share with the participants in class that life is trivial; the relationship bank will always deposit and withdraw, the focus is on a good balance, and you will enjoy a harmonious relationship.

All in all, I really enjoyed working and living with Jeson. He's very busy in high school right now, and it's a blessing for me to have the opportunity to live and work together. Without his support and help, my work would not have been able to be carried out so deeply and wonderfully. My life would not be so rich and wonderful without his companionship and love. At the same time, I am often amazed by Jeson's spirituality and transparency, intelligence and shrewdness, seriousness and responsibility, and humor. These warm moments of laughter and interaction and the deep resonance of the soul are all precious memories and treasures that I will have in this life. The relationship between us, as mother and son, as well as friends and work partner, reminds me of Kahlil Gibran's poem in "On Children" –

You may strive to be like them,
But seek not to make them like you,
For life goes not backward
Nor tarries with yesterday.

Mandy Tang

Founder of American Mental Development
Research & Education Organization

August 2024, CA, USA

前言 (Chinese Version)

源 起

经常会有人会好奇地问我："你当初为什么要学习心理学，是抑郁了吗？"

我现在想想当初走上自我成长之路的机缘，虽然谈不上抑郁，但也的确是因为不快乐。那时我还在中国，我住在还算不错的房子、开着还算不错的车、拥有一份还算不错的事业、拥有还算不错的老公和孩子，可是我依然不快乐，我不明白到底哪里出了错？

后来我去看了一两次心理辅导，辅导完了感觉其实世界原来很美好，外在哪里都没错，如果一定要找个错处，那就是我从内心看待这个世界的眼光"错了"。这一两次辅导带给我最大的好处，不仅是我找回了快乐，而是让我发现了另外一个精彩的世界——原来除了外在的声色名利的物质世界，还有一个内在的世界，这里深藏着我所有喜怒哀乐的根源。

从这里开始，我走上了自我发现之路、内在成长之路。我参加了很多心理学的课程，进入心理教育领域。这是一条幸福之路，也是我的人生使命之路。

发现

2015 年我来到美国，这里是心理科学和内在成长领域的前沿。然而我发现很多第一代移民，不论是刚刚来美的，甚至来美国几十年的老移民，他们的意识形态仍然与美国人差异很大。也许是成长在中国的来自根源的文化背景差异、也许是来美后因为语言文化等问题很难深入融入美国社会，所以，美国的前沿的心理科学和内在成长的资源，并没有太多地的被中国移民应用和吸收。

我观察到这表现出来 2 个很有趣的现象：

1.很多美国的华人一代移民，他们仍然在为人性最基本的生存需求、安全需求而奔忙，而很难追求更高层级的内在成长、自我实现等需求的实现；当然，这种现象并无高下之分，只是不同的生命状态（感谢作者 Jeson 在后面的章节中更详细的阐述了人本主义的内在需求理论，有助于大家理解此段内容）；

2.少部分人有内在成长来满足更高层级的需求，但因为语言不太通、文化不太同，又很难高效的使用美国的丰富和前沿的科学与环境资源。

我想，我有一定的心理学的专业积累、我在中国的高校曾任英语教师有英语基础、我一直在实践内在成长、有很多经验和教训，这些，都可以促成我的新梦想——我希望成为连接中美的一座心的桥梁，搭建起心理科学和内在成长的互通之路，助力更多华人活出幸福。

因为，无论在美国在中国、无论职场人士还是全职太太，幸福，难道不是每个人最终想要的吗？

筑 梦

基于这个美国之梦，我在来美国近 10 年时间，学习了很多美国本土的心理学和心灵成长课程，考取了在亲子关系、亲密关系、个人成长等领域的资格认证，并成立了非盈利机构——美国漫谈心心理发展研究与教育组织 AMDREO，针对成人和青少年，开展团体和一对一课程与辅导，将我学到的这些正源的美国课程传播给华人们，让科学的工具可以帮助大家活出更多幸福感。这些都要特别感谢我的先生在精神和物质等全方面的支持，让我可以做我喜欢的事。

我目前主要带领的课程体系，是由美国心理学家戈登博士开发的系列人际关系课程，包括"P.E.T.父母效能训练"、"Y.E.T.青少年效能训练"、"T.E.T.教师效能训练"、成为目前全美唯一一位本土获得戈登国际培训中心上述认证的执教华人讲师，我深深为此自豪。除此之外，我还带领关于亲密关系和情绪管理等专题。我的课程形式包括的成人与青少年的团体课程和一对一支持。

同时，为了更多的青少年们也能学习和应用这些科学理念与工具，我的儿子也就是本书作者 Jeson Zhang，在 2022 年发起了漫谈心青少年自我成长俱乐部 Y.S.D.C.，我作为俱乐部的总顾问，协助他一起开发了青少年自我成长公益研讨会项目。漫谈心也因此获得了美国总统义工奖官方认证机构的殊荣。

每个周末，在洛杉矶地区的几个城市，都会开展公益研讨会，青少年们就关心的自我成长主题开展研讨。本书不仅收录了研讨会中的关于"来自生活的礼物"这一主题的部分研讨报告，还收录了在 2023 年度获得美国总统义工奖的多位 Y.S.D.C.俱乐部的青少年领袖及部分家长们的成长感言。

幸 福

很多人不解，说 Mandy 你这么辛苦的讲课，又不赚什么钱，图什么啊？

也有很多人夸赞，说 Mandy 你真有大爱，不计个人得失为大家付出。

我喜欢人本主义心理学家戈登博士的理论——每个人做出某个外在行为，是因为这个行为能满足他自己的内心需求。这个大道至简的道理，帮助我看清很多真相。

所以，我做这些事，不是因为我傻，也不是因为我高尚，而是因为它满足了我的内心需求——与志同道合的学员们一起谈论内在成长话题、实现了我的社交和情感交流的需求；有更多人因为我的助力而更幸福，满足了我的成就感的需求；备课讲课与支持他人让我体验到源源不断的创造力和生命力，满足了我的自我实现的需求；学习实践和分享，让我越来越多的体验到内心世界丰富和精彩，越来越多的了解真实的自己与他人，这些都让我一直走在回归本性的幸福之路上……

因此，幸福其实很简单：了解内心，满足需求，自我负责同时又助力他人。

我可以为我的幸福做主，你，也一样可以。

礼 物

在这里，我要特别感谢本书的作者，我的儿子Jeson Zhang。他是我收获这份人生幸福礼物的天使。

感谢 Jeson 是我的宝贵的试验田。我作为一名带领亲子课程和青少年课程的讲师，如果我分享的内容我自己并没有深入地实践过，或者我没有支持青少年成长的丰富经验，那我的课程就很难有说服力。Jeson 是我重要的试验田和成长基地。在他身上，我对每一个技法使用的效果观察、每一次实践而来的心法领悟，都使得我的功力在全天候积累，即使我在青少年团体或一对一的课程上和青少年有很多很深入的接触，但都无法与 Jeson 带给我的无缝成长所比拟。在他身上，我看到人本主义养育方式带来的效果，这让我的工作更加有动力。

感谢 Jeson 是我的青少年课程的助教。他全然弥补了英语作为我的第二语言在教学中的不足，也弥补了我与青少年学员之间难免的代沟，为课程的活泼和吸引力增色太多；同时，他也是我的良师益友，他和我一起制作课程资料、为我反馈课程效果、和我讨论各种关于父母、青少年甚至人性成长的案例和话题，我也经常向他求教青少年的视角和观点。另外，他对课程内容的掌握和精彩实践，令我对课程和自己都越来越有信心。更令我欣慰的是，他创立的美国漫谈心理青少年自我成长俱乐部，不仅创造了一片他的自我成长的实践天地，也帮助更多同龄人一起成长，更使得我的助己助人的人生使命得以延续。

感谢 Jeson 是我的孩子。我和先生都在中国成人，Jeson 在美国长大，我们之间有很大差异，他听不懂我们的成语，我们听不懂他的笑话。他喜欢的明星、他玩的游戏、他听的音乐、他读的书籍等，对我们来说基本都是空白。美国的教育与社会理念和中国有很大的不同，而我们父母作为过来人，有很多我们认为正确的价值观希望他能秉承，对他也有很多期待。所以，当语言和文化如此大差异，

15

青春期又遇到更年期，即使一直都在内在成长，亲子之间也仍然都会时不时看彼此不顺眼，偶尔还会吼两嗓子。好在我们全家都一直共同学习，使用科学有效的方法，使得我们的关系银行总是余额满满。正如戈登博士所说：父母是人不是神，真实比完美更重要。我也课堂在经常和学员们分享：生活就是鸡毛蒜皮，关系银行总会存存取取，重点是余额富足，就会享受彼此圆融和谐的关系，工作学习生活都会更高效和温情。

总之，我非常享受和 Jeson 共同工作和生活的时光。他现在的高中学业十分繁忙，而我们能以此机缘不仅一起生活还能一起工作，真是我之幸事。没有他的支持和帮助，我的工作就无法如此深入和精彩的开展；没有他的陪伴和爱，我的生活就不会如此丰富精彩。同时，Jeson 的灵性和通透、聪慧与机敏、认真和负责、风趣又幽默，都经常令我叹为观止自愧弗如。我们在一起的欢笑互动的温情时光、深入灵魂的交流共鸣，都是我此生弥足珍贵的记忆、回味无穷的宝藏。在我们亦母子、亦朋友、亦工作伙伴的相处中，时时让我想起纪伯伦在"孩子"一诗中的诗句：

"你可以拼尽全力像他们一样，

但不可让他们像你，

因为生命不会倒退，

也不会滞留在往昔。"

汤漫 Mandy

美国漫谈心心理发展研究与教育组织　发起人

青少年自我成长俱乐部 总顾问

2024 年 8 月美国加州

Chapter 1: What makes you happy or unhappy?

A question to start

Imagine if I asked you, "What makes you happy?"

You may answer: "McDonald's Big Mac" or "Get a new phone."

Also, if I ask you, "What makes you unhappy?"

your answers may be "Not sleeping enough" or "I got a D on my math test."

Yes, I agree with you to some degree. I would have said the same things as you; these are also what many teenagers I know say.

However, my understanding of the source of happiness and unhappiness deepened when I had the privilege of leading many of the Youth Effectiveness Training workshops as a teacher's assistant and founding the Youth Self-Development Club in California in 2022. (Thanks to my mom, Mandy, a psychology educator and the founder of a non-profit organization, American Mental Development Research & Education Organization. I would not say it's lucky or not for me to have such a busy mom).

What psychologists and teenagers say

I first heard about the theory of the source of happiness in the Youth Effectiveness Training workshop developed by American Humanistic Psychologist Dr. Thomas Gordon.

Dr. Gordon has accomplished a remarkable life. He was nominated for the Nobel Peace Prize three times and named the "Father of Communication." He was the Children's adviser to the United States White House and received the American Psychological Association's Lifetime Achievement Award. His accolades are too numerous to mention.

I worked as a teaching assistant for many Y.E.T. workshops. These theories and tools helped me understand myself and promote relationships. At the same time, I wonder if they can also work for other teenagers. I know that in the Parent Effectiveness Training workshop (a homogeneous workshop from Dr. Gordon for parents), led by my mom for almost seven years, the feedback from the participants was that the tools were very effective. The book also includes several pieces of feedback from parents.

So, I started a non-profit Youth Self-Development Club. I've picked out some simple tools from Dr. Gordon's public publications (also in the Y.E.T. workshop) for the youth self-development seminars so that more teenagers will learn and apply these tools through seminars and can see the effects.

The seminars, held every weekend across five cities in California, focus on issues pressing to current teenagers and how to solve them with Dr. Gordon's tools. For example, the topics are what makes you happy or unhappy, how to manage yourself, how to deal with bullying at school, how to find a new hobby, how to make money, etc. We have over 500 research reports in the last three years.

Through these seminar research reports and Dr. Gordon's and other psychologists' insights, we determined what makes someone happy or unhappy. Happiness is not caused by outside behavior, such as eating a Big Mac, but rather by inner needs. An inner need is a desire that drives one to an outside behavior.

We can understand this conclusion more intuitively from Maslow's Hierarchy of Needs.

Maslow, a person-centered psychologist like Gordon, concluded the five levels of inside needs (see image underneath). Eating a Big Mac satisfies your physiological needs, thus making you happy. You are unhappy when you get a D in math, possibly because your mom will cut your Wi-Fi, and your need for socializing (Belongingness and love needs) cannot be reached, or you feel like you've put in a lot of effort but haven't met your expectations, your Esteem needs are not satisfied, or What's worse, maybe your dad will kick your ass, your safety needs won't be met. I'm pretty sure you won't be happy.

Maslow's Hierarchy of Needs

Maslow's Hierarchy of Needs

A Trap of "Inner Need"

Here is a point often confusing about inner needs: the external things and not our inner needs; they are solutions to our needs. For example, what need not be met if you lose a tennis match and are angry? You may think of a new ticket. (This example is true; it comes from our seminar research report) No, your need is not a new tennis racket, but to win a tournament, your Self-esteem Needs, and even boast to your classmates about how amazing you are, your Belongingness, and love needs). The new tennis racket is an external solution that may help you win the game, satisfy your inner needs, and make you happy. On the contrary, if you do not win the match with the new racket, you will not be happy and will even hate and smash the tennis racket. So, it's not the new tennis racket that brings you joy; you're satisfying your esteem and beloved needs.

In conclusion, I agree with Dr. Gordon and even humanism: You are happy because your inner needs are met. Unhappiness comes from your needs not being met. It's as simple as that.

Knowing the Needs, More Benefits

So, what are the benefits of understanding this theory?

(1) Self-responsible. We make ourselves happy by satisfying our needs and not basing our happiness on external things or other people.

For example, I realize I am unhappy when I lose in a tennis match because my need to succeed is not fulfilled. I will not blame the trial as unfair; the opponent was too strong, and the coach didn't give me the right guidance. Maybe these are the truths, but I can choose not to complain when I'm self-responsible. My happiness is decided by my needs being met. Others are not responsible for my happiness. So, if I want my need for accomplishment satisfied through tennis, I cannot change others but myself. All I can do is put my efforts into my own actions, such as practicing tennis more diligently or trying to communicate with the trial or coach, and make me happy by taking responsibility for my needs.

(2) Let others decide their happiness. This is good news for those who want to take life easy. Whether others are happy or unhappy depends on whether their needs are met. I'd love to help him,

but I'm not the one to be responsible for his happiness.

For instance, my friend complained about the new teacher because he thought the class was boring. I like this teacher because he allows us to look up information independently, which allows me to think quietly. I know that my friend is unhappy just because his need for a fun class is unmet. There is no right or wrong for the needs. I will not judge and push him to be happy with the teacher; I can share why I like the teacher and leave the responsibility for his happiness to himself. I'm easy; he's easy.

(3) More possibilities, More happiness. If we understand our inner needs, we find many other solutions to meet them, and our world becomes more open.

If my need is self-esteem, in tennis, I can not only concentrate on winning and losing but also pay attention to small accomplishments to meet my needs, like playing a good game that I couldn't do before. I can also observe other achievements, like getting an A on today's math test. All of these fulfill my need for self-esteem and make me happy. My little progress is everywhere, just waiting for me to discover it.

(4) Improving relationship. When I understand the need theory, I want to help satisfy others' needs and make them happy because I value our relationship. Of course, if there are good relationships, it will be much easier to be successful when I have to meet my needs with the help of others; this happens quite often.

For example, I like to listen to music when I do my homework, and my brother, who lives in the same room, likes to be quiet. Conflict will inevitably arise if I don't consider his needs and only look out for mine. So, I bring headphones and listen to music to meet the needs of both of us, and everyone is happy. We have a good relationship, so the next time we have a conflict, I am sure he will more likely consider my needs.

Therefore, it is imperative to understand each other's needs. Our Y.S.D.C. seminar has a program named "The Gifts from My Life," which is focused on when something happens, you feel happy or unhappy, practicing being aware of your needs and what you did or will do to meet them. I will put some of those in the book for reference.

Happy or not, I'll decide.

Through these humanistic theories and the practice at the seminars, we find that whether our experiences are happy or unhappy, if we are aware of them, they are gifts from life that allow us to learn more about our needs and discover more solutions to meet them. By being self-responsible and collaborating with others, we can be happier and help others be happier.

Our lives are created by ourselves.

是什么令你快乐和不快乐?

先来回答一个小问题

想象一下,如果我问你, "什么让你快乐? "

你可能会回答: "麦当劳的巨无霸" 或 "买一部新手机"。

此外,如果我问你 "是什么让你不开心",

你的回答可能是 "睡眠不足" 或 "我的数学考试得了 D"。

是的,你在某种程度上是对的,我也会这样回答,这些也是我认识的许多青少年的答案。

然而,当我作为教师助理,带领多期 "Y.E.T.青少年效能训练" 工作坊,并于 2022 年在加州创立 "青少年自我发展俱乐部" Y.S.D.C. 后,我对快乐和不快乐来源的理解加深了。 (这得感谢我有个心理培训师的妈妈 Mandy,她也是非盈利机构 "美国漫谈心心理发展与教育组织" 的发起人。我不会跟你讨论有这样一个闲不住的妈妈对我来说是幸运还是不幸。)

心理学家和青少年们怎么说？

我第一次听说幸福来源的理论，是在美国人本主义心理学家托马斯·戈登（Thomas Gordon）博士开发的"Y.E.T.青少年效能训练"工作坊上。

戈登博士成就了非凡的一生。他曾三次获得诺贝尔和平奖提名，并被誉为"传播学之父"。他曾是美国白宫的儿童顾问，并获得了美国心理学会的终身成就奖。他的荣誉不胜枚举。

我曾在许多期 Y.E.T.工作坊上担任助教。这些理论和工具帮助我了解自己并促进人际关系。同时，我想知道他们是否也对其他青少年有效果。我知道在我妈妈作为导师带领的"P.E.T.父母效能训练"工作坊中，（这是戈登博士针对父母开发的同系列课程），参加的父母们的反馈是这些工具非常有效，本书也收录了一些父母们的反馈。

于是，我成立了一个非营利性的青少年自我发展俱乐部 Y.S.D.C.。我从戈登博士的公共出版物中挑选了一些简单的工具（也是在 Y.E.T.工作坊中的内容），设计了青少年自我发展研讨会，以便更多的青少年通过研讨会学习和应用这些简单工具，从而能收集到效果。

每周末在美国加州几个城市的研讨会中，青少年们都会聚焦于当前同龄人关心的问题，以及如何使用戈登博士的工具解决这些问题。例如，是什么令你快乐或不快乐、怎样自我管理、怎样面对校园霸凌、如何找到新的爱好、以及如何赚钱等。到现在近三年时间里，我们在这些研讨会上收到了 500 多份来自青少年的研讨报告。

我们通过这些研讨报告和戈登博士等人本主义心理学家的见解，确定了什么让人快乐或不快乐。令人惊讶的是：快乐不快乐不是由外界决定的（例如吃麦当劳巨无霸），而是由内在需求决定的。需求是一种驱使一个人做出外在行为的欲望。

我们可以从马斯洛的需求层次理论中更直观地理解这个结论。

马斯洛，和戈登博士一样都是人本主义心理学家，他总结了内心需求的五个层次（见下图）。吃巨无霸可以满足你的生理需求和美味的需求，从而让你快乐。当你数学得 D 时，你会不高兴，可能是因为你的妈妈会切断你的 WIFI，使你的社交需求无法得到满足；或者你觉得自己付出很多却没达成预期，你对成就感/尊重的需求没有得到满足；也或者更糟糕是爸爸会因此踢你的屁股，你的安全需求无法得到满足，那我敢肯定你一定高兴不起来。

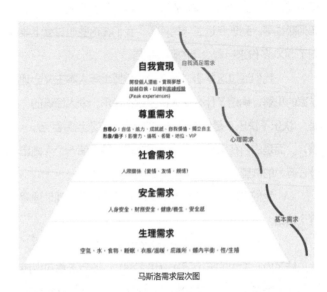

马斯洛需求层次图

关于"需求"的小陷阱

这里有一个关于需求很容易混淆的小陷阱我们需要区分清楚：外在事物不是你的需求(Need)，它们是满足你需求的解决方案(Solution)。比如，如果你输了网球比赛，你很生气，是因为你的什么需求没有满足呢？

你可能会说你的需求是一个新的网球拍（这是个真实的例子，来自于我们青少年研讨会报告）。 不，你的需求不是一个新的网球拍，而是赢得比赛(自我价值感的需求)、可以跟同学夸耀你多棒（归属感和爱的需求）。新的网球拍是一个外在的解决方案，可以帮助你赢得比赛，满足你的内心你需求使你快乐。相反，如果你使用了新网球拍却并没有赢得比赛，你会不高兴，甚至会恨甚至会砸新网球拍。所以，并不是新网球拍带给你快乐或不快乐，而是你赢得比赛的成就感和被爱的内心需求被满足带来了快乐。

总之，我很同意戈登博士乃至人本主义的洞见——你快乐是因为你的内在需求得到了满足，不快乐是因为你的内在需求没有得到满足。就这么简单。

对我有什么用？

那么，理解了这个理论可以给我们带来什么好处呢？

（1）学会对我自己的快乐负责。我们通过满足自己的内在需求来获得幸福，而不是将快乐建立在外在事物或他人身上。

例如，当我输了网球比赛时，我意识到我不快乐，是因为我成就感的需求没有得到满足。我就不会责怪裁判不公平、球拍旧了、对手太强、或教练没给我正确的指导等等。也许这些是事实，但是当我自我负责时，我会理解但不抱怨。我的快乐是由我的需求得到满足决定的，别人并不对我高兴不高兴负责。所以，如果我想通过网球比赛来满足我对成就感的需求，我无法改变别人，只能改变自己，我所能做的是把我的努力放在网球练习、或尝试和裁判或教练沟通等我的自主行为上，通过自我负责满足我的需求，让我感到快乐。

（2）让别人来决定他的快乐。对于那些想要轻松生活的人来说，这是个好消息。别人是快乐还是不快乐，取决于他们的需求是否得到满足。我很乐意帮助他来满足他的需求，但我不是那个对他的快乐负责的人。

例如，我的好朋友跟我抱怨新老师，因为他觉得新老师的课堂很无聊。而我喜欢这位老师，因为老师让我们独立查找信息，满足了我安静思考的需求。我知道我的好朋友不高兴，只是因为他喜欢有趣的课堂体验的需求没有得到满足。需求并没有对错之分。我不会评判他，也不会强迫他一定要对新老师感到高兴，我可以分享我喜欢老师的原因，我把他快乐或不快乐的责任留给他自己。我很轻松，他也很轻松。

（3）更多可能，更多快乐。如果我们理解了内在需求，就会发现满足这个需求的外在解决方案其实有很多，我们的世界变得有更多开放的可能性。

仍然是网球的例子，除了关注输赢，我也有更多的方式来满足自我成就感价值感，比如关注一些小的进步，打了一个以前从没打过的好球等。或者也可以聚焦其他的外在解决方案，比如今天数学考了 A 等等。总之，我的小进步有很多，都可以满足自我实现的需求，只等我来发现。

（4）促进关系。当我们明白需求理论后，我们也可以帮助满足他人的需求来让他们快乐，因为我重视我们之间的关系。当然，很多时候我们必须通过别人的帮助来满足我的需求，如果有好的关系，我就会更容易获得他人帮助。

比如，我做作业的时候喜欢听音乐，而住在同一个房间的弟弟喜欢安静。如果我不考虑他的需求，只关注我的需求，就不可避免地会有冲突。于是，我带上耳机，既可以听音乐又不打扰弟弟，从而满足我们双方的需求，大家都很开心。这样我就给我们的关系银行存钱进去，我和弟弟的关系就因此更好，所以下次当我和他又有了冲突时，我相信他也会更容易考虑我的需求。

因此，了解彼此的内心需求非常重要。我们的青少年自我成长研讨会专门有一个名为"来自我生命中的礼物"的主题项目，同学们会讨论在日常学习和生活中，有哪些令你快乐的事，哪些令你不快乐的事，并练习觉察内心需求，以及可以做些什么来满足这些需求。我将把其中的一些青少年们的研讨内容放在书中作为参考。

幸福不幸福，我说了算

通过这些人本主义的经验和青少年自我成长研讨会上的讨论实践，我发现，无论我们的经历是快乐还是不快乐，如果我们意识到它们，就会知道，它们都是来自生活的礼物，可以让我们更多地了解自己的需求，发现更多的解决方案来满足需求。通过自我负责和与他人协作，我们可以更快乐，也可以帮助别人更快乐。

我们的生活状态是由我们自己创造的。

Chapter 2: The Gifts from My Life

"The Gift from My Life" is a big theme in our Youth Self-Development Seminar, in which we discuss and share what has happened recently that makes me happy and unhappy and be aware of my inner needs and how they can help me meet them. This chapter includes some seminar presentations to help readers understand the inner world of teenagers and their self-development journeys.

"来自生活的礼物"是我们青少年自我成长研讨会中的一个大主题，在这个主题下，每次研讨会，大家会讨论和分享近期发生的令我开心的事和不开心的事，并借此觉察内心的需求，和怎样可以帮助我满足这些需求。本章收录了一些研讨会报告，帮助读者了解青少年的内心世界，和青少年自我成长的心路历程。

2.1 The Gifts from My Happiness

The Gifts from My Happiness (1)

Name	Charlie
Situation	Yesterday, at home with my friends, my Microsoft account got hacked, but I was able to regain control through the appeal form. I am still waiting to secure the account.
Feeling	I felt extremely relieved and almost became religious over an unnecessarily stressful event.
Needs	Protection and freedom from fear because I believe the account breach constituted a risk to my security, as my Microsoft account could be potentially linked to some very important and personal information.
What did you do	I worked hard to stay calm and control my stress, and by tirelessly trying to resolve the issue, I managed to fix it somewhat. I resolved the need in this case by just finishing the task. I worked hard to stay calm and control my stress, and by tirelessly trying to resolve the issue, I managed to fix it somewhat. I resolved the need in this case by just finishing the task.
Insights	It is very important for people to record their experiences of hardship and share them with others; there is no point in making someone go through a problem alone when easier methods have already been discovered by others.

The Gifts from My Happiness (2)

Name	Jialin
Situation	Yesterday, at home, I ate delicious food.
Feeling	I was relaxed and happy.
Needs	Relax and belong because when I'm relaxed, it gives me a chance to be happy, and I don't have to be worried anymore.
What did you do	Get rid of my stress and enjoy the time after it with people I talk to.
Insights	Ideas of how I could have a better mood and be happy. Try methods concluded today in the future and apply them in daily life.

The Gifts from My Happiness (3)

Name	Jiayi
Situation	At a party last weekend, with a new friend and both our parents, we told each other our names.
Feeling	I felt happy and lucky since I found a friend who is really friendly and we have similar personalities.
Needs	Friendship and not to be lonely because we have the same interests and similar personalities so that we can get along well with each other.
What did you do	We shared our experiences with one another and became friends soon after we found we were similar people to my friends and the people surrounding me.
Insights	Talking to others positively is very important. We can't just wait for someone to come and talk to you. Trying to find a topic that both of you are interested in so that you can avoid nothing to talk about.

The Gifts from My Happiness (4)

Name	Johnson
Situation	Last week, in an art class, a guy handled the ink I needed.
Feeling	I appreciate his performance and am excited to make a friend.
Needs	Belonging because he grabbed me the ink I needed, I think it's the need to belong.
What did you do	I might have said thanks to him. Actually, it's hard to say that I did something.
Insights	To be helpful to others is a good way to make friends (I learned it from that guy). Otherwise, you can wait until somebody comes and helps you. But that's not going to be effective.

The Gifts from My Happiness (5)

Name	Youyou
Situation	During the first week of classes, at school with other friends, it was my first time going to high school, and I just met my teachers and classmates.
Feeling	I have learned along the way that building friendships is a rewarding journey that can enrich lives. Connections through shared interests, meaningful conversations, and mutual respect are the cornerstones of true friendship. It's about supporting during challenging times, celebrating successes, and enjoying shared experiences that build lasting connections.
Needs	Respecting others improves my relationship with teachers and peers because I value my grades very much and try every means to improve them to a level that I am satisfied with.
What did you do	Respecting others improves my relationship with teachers and peers because I value my grades very much and try every means to improve them to a level that I am satisfied with. I take the initiative to liven up the atmosphere in various activities and be the first to introduce myself to my classmates and teachers.
Insights	In expanding and handling interpersonal relationships or increasing our favorability, we should respect and actively communicate. You need to have enough confidence and courage to be more likable.

The Gifts from My Happiness (6)

Name	Melody
Situation	Friday, at Long Beach, with my friend, we saw the sunset together and took many really pretty pictures.
Feeling	Relaxed, happy
Needs	I need to release my stress because I have a lot of stuff going on, and I have an essay next week and many quizzes next week.
What did you do	I was relaxed and with my friends to take pictures of the sunset.
Insights	I learned how to be relaxed with nature because it helps give me the energy to relax.

The Gifts from My Happiness (7)

Name	Clover
Situation	This Wednesday, at home with my family, I got a new iPhone.
Feeling	Excited
Needs	I want to have something more convenient with more storage so I can save many more videos and photos on my phone.
What did you do	I will pay for it, but my dad bought the line.
Insights	I have to start saving money.

The Gifts from My Happiness (8)

Name	Jeson
Situation	Last night, I finished the main story of Red Dead Redemption II, a video game, after 65 hours total.
Feeling	Happy, proud, and sad
Needs	To have fun, feel proud of myself, and feel accomplished because it was the longest mission I have played.
What did you do	I spent 65 hours concentrating on the game with the door closed so I was not disturbed. I finished all of my work so I would not be bothered.
Insights	I can accomplish something if I give it enough time and dedication.

The Gifts from My Happiness (9)

Name	Eric
Situation	Last Friday, at school, I didn't fail my test.
Feeling	Relief because it was hard.
Needs	Happiness, not suffering because my parents will scream at me and take away all my privileges and send me out of the house if I fail.
What did you do	I reviewed for the test with the help of my computer so as not to fail it.
Insights	I need to spend more time to fulfill my needs.

The Gifts from My Happiness (10)

Name	Keelia
Situation	Last Monday, at home, the sign-ups for the seminars on the weekend filled up in five minutes.
Feeling	Pride, excitement
Needs	Helping others and being welcomed as a leader during the seminars.
What did you do	I tried my best during every seminar, followed the rules, and organized ice-breaker games.
Insights	I must take everything seriously to feel better about myself and help others.

2.2 The Gifts from My Unhappiness

The Gifts from My Unhappiness (1)

Name	Sunny
Situation	November last year, at school by myself, I couldn't complete all 11 journals for my English assignment, but I needed to complete them, or else it was late work. I would rather lose 40% of my grade than have half of it taken away.
Feeling	Disappointed because I will receive a low grade that will impact my report card grade. I'm a bit peeved about the teacher assigning so much homework before Christmas break. Let me rest; I'm not a machine that does 11 journals in 5 days. I got other stuff to do like tennis, reading club, etc.
Unmet needs	self-actualization: I need more time to finish my homework because I have many things to do, plus my math homework was so difficult that it took me half my homework time to complete. I couldn't finish all the journals, but I needed to finish them ASAP, so I wrote whatever came out of my head. I cannot set my goals to an unreachable limit. I hope the English teacher will not assign this much homework in the second semester.
If this happens again	If the situation happens again, I will seek help from my advisor and English teacher, finish English homework first, and then do other things. These people can ensure I'm on track with my work, and during the tutorials, I can have a conference with my teacher to review my writing. Then, I will receive feedback and revise my work. By asking for help, I can realize that I can push myself beyond my thoughts of limits.
Insights	I will check in with my English teacher about assignment deadlines, finish English homework first, and ask for help when necessary.

The Gifts from My Unhappiness (2)

Name	Celia
Situation	During winter break, at home by myself, my guinea pig fell from the table.
Feeling	I felt very sad. I wanted to take him to the vet ASAP.
Unmet needs	Protection because I didn't care for him enough, so he fell from the table. If I look after him carefully, he won't break his bone. So, I have to take care of him more and give him medicine.
If this happens again	If that situation happens again, I will take him to the vet and get more professional help. Also, I will take care of him more carefully and ask my mom to take him to the vet. I can ask other friends and get better help for my Guinea pig.
Insights	I will care for him more carefully and help them get better. He is getting better after recovering from his condition these few days.

The Gifts from My Unhappiness (3)

Name	Aimmy
Situation	Today, at home with my friend, we can't exchange gifts on Monday because Abby is sick.
Feeling	I feel very sad because I can't give and get my gift.
Unmet needs	Happiness and friendship because I really wanted to get my gift since we planned this last month, and there were so many delays.
If this happens again	Double-check ahead of time with my friends because without them, it wouldn't happen.
Insights	I learned about time and about delays

The Gifts from My Unhappiness (4)

Name	Lingyi
Situation	Right now, here, I have a really hard chemistry test tomorrow, and I spent the whole day with my friends, so I will have a hard time finishing the five assignments from chemistry and studying.
Feeling	I feel stressed, nervous, worried, and tired.
Unmet needs	I do not have enough time to do all my homework because I was irresponsible and should've finished most of my homework yesterday, but I didn't.
If this happens again	I would do my homework earlier with better time management.
Insights	I learned that I should not procrastinate. Also, I should stop watching YouTube while I do my homework because that makes me slower.

The Gifts from My Unhappiness (5)

Name	Alex
Situation	Today, at church with myself, I ate five pizzas and felt really full.
Feeling	Sad because I thought I was wasting food, and I could've donated the food to people starving in Africa.
Unmet needs	Self-actualization because I ate too much, and it was a waste of food, and I could've fed people with the food.
If this happens again	If this happens again, then I will become sad and think of myself as selfish. I could get help from a friend to stop me from eating too much pizza.
Insights	I learned that I should be more thoughtful when it comes to waste.

The Gifts from My Unhappiness (6)

Name	Ryan
Situation	Last week, at Sonora High School, my teammates and I lost our basketball match.
Feeling	Impartial, disappointed
Unmet needs	Winning, self-accomplishment because I lost, and losing isn't winning, which makes me disappointed.
If this happens again	I could be better at basketball and not get outmatched, and practice with a coach can help me improve.
Insights	I have to write my problems out.

The Gifts from My Unhappiness (7)

Name	Luna
Situation	Friday, at school, with my teacher, she assigned a judge project over break.
Feeling	Mad
Needs	Rest and relax. I deserve a break, but I cannot have a good break.
If this happens again	Fight the teacher with my entire friend group. I could also complain to someone.
Insights	I learned that teachers are cruel and mean.

The Gifts from My Unhappiness (8)

Name	Clover
Situation	Friday, at home with my dad, we got into an argument.
Feeling	Hurt
Unmet needs	Good relationships and focus because I was under huge stress, and my brain stopped letting me have the motivation to study.
If this happens again	Be more motivated with my friends.
Insights	I learned how to deal with my unhappiness better and how to motivate myself.

The Gifts from My Unhappiness (9)

Name	Melody
Situation	Yesterday, at school, with my teacher, my teacher graded my test wrong, and she won't give me the points back.
Feeling	Sad, heartbreaking
Unmet needs	Self-accomplishment because my math teacher won't give me my deserved grade
If this happens again	I will try to work harder and not wait until the last moment to study for my test , and I will probably report my math teacher to the principal. I could also ask my mom to help me report the math teacher.
Insights	I learned that be nice to your teacher only if they are nice.

The Gifts from My Unhappiness (10)

Name	Keelia
Situation	Friday, at school, with Amy, I realized that I have a science test on Monday
Feeling	Anxious, scared, stressed
Unmet needs	Peace and relaxation. I wanted Monday to be a peaceful and stressless day, my science teacher made a test on microwaves.
If this happens again	I would ask my teacher ahead of time so as to not be surprised when an assessment occurs.
Insights	I learned to not procrastinate.

Chapter 3: The Milestones on the Road of Self-Development

The Youth Self-Development seminars have changed many youths. The following is a collection of statements from the President's Volunteer Service Award 2023 winners in AMDREO, including seminar leaders and participants.

青少年自我成长研讨会给很多青少年带来了改变。本章收录了在美国漫谈心心理发展研究与教育组织获得 2023 年度"美国总统义工奖"的青少年们的收获，其中有带领研讨会的领袖，也有参加者。

Making a Difference

Keelia Cao

My name is Keelia Cao, and I am honored to participate in the Youth Self-Development Club (YSDC). Our club addresses mental and physical issues through collaborative seminars and action plans. Here, I want to share my experiences, how I have contributed, and the impact of these activities on myself and others.

During our volunteer activities at YSDC, I helped organize and facilitate seminars addressing various mental and physical health challenges faced by youth. My responsibilities included preparing educational materials, leading discussions, and assisting in creating personalized action plans for participants. I also provided one-on-one support to those needing additional guidance.

One key aspect of our seminars is providing direct support to participants. During a seminar on stress management, I noticed a participant struggling with anxiety. Using the techniques we discussed, such as deep breathing exercises and time management strategies, I offered personalized advice. Over the following weeks, she reported feeling more in control and less overwhelmed.

Another participant, who faced issues with self-esteem, benefited from the positive reinforcement techniques we practiced, helping him gain confidence and participate more actively.

Being involved in YSDC has profoundly impacted me. One significant change is my improved public speaking skills. Leading seminars and facilitating group discussions have made me more comfortable and articulate in front of an audience. Additionally, the experience of helping others has increased my empathy and understanding. Witnessing positive changes in participants' lives, such as improved mental health and increased confidence, has been incredibly rewarding and motivating.

The feedback from my family, teachers, and friends has been overwhelmingly positive. My family has noticed that I am more empathetic and patient. Teachers have commented on my enhanced leadership abilities and commitment to helping others. Friends have mentioned that I seem more confident and capable of handling stress, attributing these changes to my involvement with YSDC.

Being part of YSDC has been a transformative experience. It has allowed me to help others and fostered my personal growth. The sense of community and support within the club is invaluable. Seeing the tangible impact of our work, such as participants reporting reduced stress levels and improved physical health, reinforces our importance. I am grateful for the opportunity to contribute to such meaningful work and look forward to continuing my journey with YSDC.

In conclusion, my time with YSDC has been filled with learning, growth, and the joy of helping others. The skills and experiences I have gained are invaluable, and I am proud to be part of a club that makes a real difference in people's lives. Thank you for this opportunity, and I am excited to see what we can achieve together in the future.

Mental Health Appreciation

Melody Jin

Volunteering at YSDC has always been a rewarding and meaningful experience for me. Throughout our activities, I have learned a lot about teenage mental health and developed many valuable skills. In this essay, I would like to share how it has impacted both myself and those around me.

In our volunteer activities, we engaged in a variety of tasks. We watched informative sources, such as videos, to understand more about teenage mental health. We discussed these topics, brainstormed ideas, and shared our thoughts with each other, gaining valuable insights to improve mental health. Together, we set plans and give feedback after a certain time. This collaborative process developed my understanding and taught me the importance of teamwork and communication.

Although I did not take on a leadership role during the seminars, I applied what I learned at the seminars to help my friends at school. For example, when my friends felt left out and self-conscious because of negative comments from others, I encouraged them not to let these words affect them. I reminded them not to care about others' negative comments and to appreciate their own worth and the good things in their lives. This helped boost their confidence and improve their self-esteem. Also, by sharing the strategies we discussed during our volunteer activities, I helped my friends see things from a more positive perspective, stay in a good mood, and vent their stress and anxiety in a healthy way.

Additionally, I have also experienced personal growth through volunteering. For example, I learned the importance of keeping promises, making me more dependable. My family noticed this change and praised me for being more responsible.

I also learned the importance of self-care. By understanding that taking care of my mental and physical health is essential, I started setting time for activities like reading, writing a diary, and painting while listening to an audiobook that helped me relax. This has improved my overall well-being.

Furthermore, volunteering taught me how to maintain healthy relationships. By learning to communicate effectively and respect others' boundaries, I have built stronger and more meaningful connections with my friends and especially my family. My friends have noticed how I have become a better listener and more empathetic, which has made our relationships more supportive and positive.

While maintaining a healthy relationship, another skill I gained is planning. Throughout setting plans for our volunteer activities, I learned how to organize my life, set descriptive plans, and manage my time better. This has helped me balance my studies, volunteer work, and personal life more effectively. I also learned to give feedback after executing the plan, which is really important for the seminar and myself.

Lastly, the feedback from my family and friends was very encouraging. My parents have noticed that I am more organized and responsible at home. My friends appreciate my support and advice, which has strengthened our friendships. Overall, they all believe that volunteering has a very positive effect on me.

In conclusion, volunteering at YSDC has provided me with an amazing and brilliant experience. Through these experiences, I have come to appreciate the importance of mental health and the impact that small acts of kindness and support can have on individuals. Volunteering has taught me that my role is still valuable and significant even though I might not be in a leadership position. It has given me the confidence to continue making a difference, no matter how small it may seem. YSDC has also offered me an excellent opportunity to help others and grow personally in ways I never thought possible. The skills and knowledge I have gained are priceless, and I am sincerely grateful for the chance to make a positive impact on my life and the lives of others. I am excited to continue volunteering and further develop myself while helping others.

Helping People to Help Myself

Alex Jin

Helping other teenagers, both younger and older than me, has been the greatest and most rewarding experience I've had thus far. I highly recommend this experience. I am so grateful for the opportunity.

This volunteer program requires that I work with a team to prepare for a seminar that has invited students in grades 6th through 12th. Leaders set up the Google Sheets and the video for the seminar, and we created name tags for people to recall each other's names easily. This seems to help incorporate a more comfortable environment for all who are invited and those in charge of the seminar. Our seminar goals and topics are decided by our team. We prepare the agenda for the seminar and work as a team to organize a positive and constructive setting for our participants. We want them to feel comfortable. Such topics are how to manage time, handle bullying, and identify types of criticism.

During each seminar, we begin with an icebreaker. We proceeded to a video that involved the topic at hand. A question-and-answer segment follows. At these seminars, I have helped others by guiding the participants in finding solutions to their problems. One example of such a problem that one teenager faced was not realizing the difference between constructive and destructive criticism. Another problem they have faced is the inability to stop bullying. Simply writing and sharing everything that has been going on with other people has benefited both other participants with certain problems and me. Some examples of the changes participants may have made could be becoming calmer in dealing with heated situations, issues with friends and families, making good habits and breaking bad ones, finding new and reliable friends, etc.

These volunteer activities have assisted me in processing thoughts during difficult and tight situations. They have also helped me learn how to keep my composure and even deal with events that seem out of my reach to change. An example would be when I was trained to become a leader. Although I had various habits to change and a lot of information to remember, I slowly got used to the concept of social interactions. This, in turn, has helped me mature. It has even helped my parents not to fight as much. When they have arguments, this training has allowed me the opportunity to intervene and halt the situation. I've offered choices to help with the resolution of the argument. They have come to the realization that my intervention techniques do work and have used them on their own to resolve situations that arise.

Some feedback I have received from my parents is that after I have completed the Y.E.T. training and actively participated in most of these volunteer activities, I have matured greatly. I have shown much more emotional control over myself when a problem appears. They also said my mood has not been as agitated as before, especially since I'm a troublemaking teenager. I have been more patient and forgiving with other people. My teacher has also emailed my parents about how I have matured and that she can see a visible change in my actions. She mentioned examples such as being more still and not as rowdy as I might have been or even just acting better and nicer to other people.

I want to thank our instructor, Mandy, for helping me mature and my fellow peers for always helping me in difficult situations. I also want to thank my parents for always being there and supporting me.

Improving My Communication Skills

Lingyi Weng

Like most other members of this Self-Development Club, my mom found a promotion of this on her WeChat app. Going in, I had no idea what to expect. Maybe a psychology experiment with empty white walls like a doctor's office? Or maybe like a college lecture hall where teens monotonously listened to a speaker while typing notes on their computer. However, I found a community of open-minded teenagers going through the same struggles in life. Every week, we had meetings around a large discussion table. We would share our thoughts and describe our problems. The members were always understanding, empathetic, and friendly. The prompts were thought-provoking and brought up important factors in my life that I had never considered before the experience.

The most important thing this volunteer experience brought me was a community of kids. Some were my age, some were a bit younger, and some were a bit older. As we spent more time together, joking, laughing, and eating snacks, we also gained an understanding of each other's personalities. Some kids were quiet, some were outgoing from the beginning, and many got out of their shells. Every day, we brought in our laptops and opened up a Google sheet pre-planned with different prompts. The leaders led us through interesting discussions, each teaching us to improve our lifestyles. Some of these included "Dealing With Racism," "Time Management," and "What To Do When You're Crushing."

One of the most helpful aspects of these seminars was when participants provided feedback to each other. For example, our problem, given the topic, would first be described. Then, we would go around sharing our problems. Some people would agree or build off of that. The leaders, specifically, would give a lot of advice on these problems. One series in our seminars called "Gifts From My Life" allowed us to share positive and negative things. Many of the people shared problems with their teachers. One of the participants had trouble in their school. They had a really difficult teacher, and I think I gave them solid advice on how to deal with those pressures. Especially as an older participant, I think giving younger teenagers pieces of wisdom gained throughout the years is pretty helpful.

We often watch videos that give examples to help solve our problems. This allowed me to face my problem directly and is the main source of my motivation. Once, we watched a video listing suggestions to improve our habits. I wanted to feel less stressed and decrease procrastination. After describing these problems and watching the video, I formulated a plan to direct my focus on one project since doing multiple will make me overwhelmed and unfocused. I also learned about balancing having fun and being productive.

These are all things that I shared with my friends at school. Even though they did not participate in the volunteer club, this seminar also gave them some new ideas to help them throughout their lives. According to my mom, this self-development club has changed the way I communicate my thoughts and views to them. For example, I can stand up for my brothers when they are being punished for something that may not be completely right.

The meeting's discussions allowed me to present my views to my parents in a way they can understand and agree to. This has been one of the crucial skills I've gained through the Youth Self-Development Club.

Helping Others and Improving Myself

Felicia Lee

Through the Youth Self-Development Club of the American Mental Development Research & Education Organization, I have been fortunate enough to partake in seminars to develop my personal growth and positively impact others. During volunteer activities, I have utilized my Youth Effectiveness Training by Dr. Thomas Gordon to help advance discussions on various mental health and self-discovery topics. I shared my opinions while staying respectful and open-minded, further fostering the exchange of ideas. By providing my thoughts, I found personal benefits while helping others find solutions and contributing additional insight into their problems. Through collaboration with club members, problems have been solved, steps have been taken to reach goals, and conflicts have been resolved. Not only do I use the techniques learned during the seminar, but I also find them helpful when discussing with leaders before and after a seminar. After noticing conflicts during the seminar, the approach was calm and appropriate, allowing everyone to speak their thoughts and avoiding misunderstandings.

Helping others in the seminar gives me a deeper understanding and different perspectives of one situation. Others maintaining an open mind while dealing with conflicts allowed me to provide my interpretation of the problem and brainstorm various solutions. While someone could have little experience on a topic, I might have gone through the situation many times, allowing me to provide knowledge and constructive advice. Much like debugging a program, collaboration can increase productivity and efficiency, as a different outlook supplies new solutions. As an illustration, forming strong friendships can be a hardship for many. Together, with active listening, I can provide support to help them reach their goals while staying neutral. Through the seminars, topics such as time management and focus were discussed. Many of my friends at school have trouble managing their time well, with the abundance of extracurriculars they are enrolled in. When my friends reported that my advice helped them, I felt proud and eager to help others. From the seminars, I supplied advice when they asked, allowing me to reflect on the topic simultaneously.

Additionally, debriefs at the end of each seminar enable leaders to work together to reflect and improve in lacking areas, improving my problem-solving and collaboration skills. If there are disagreements with no apparent solution, compromises have been made to provide the best experience for the participants. Through the debriefs, I have been exposed to the importance of flexibility and adaptability, two important qualities needed in many different settings. If participants feel that improvements are needed, the leaders work together with the participants to try to accommodate their needs. When something agreed upon is ineffective, participants are open to giving suggestions to increase the quality of the seminar.

My parents have noticed a few improvements since I started attending seminars. My mom reported that I have started listening and considering others' ideas more when dealing with personal problems. Some topics like time and money management have never been at the top of my mind, but due to the seminars, I have had the opportunity to learn about them. There have been times when I have struggled to sleep earlier and the problem and solution became apparent when I learned more about time management.

Throughout the volunteer activities, I have noticed personal growth and an increased ability to tune in and help others. Not only did the seminars help me, but they also allowed me to help others and make a positive difference. Whenever I help someone else, I feel a sense of motivation and fulfillment, fueling me with a desire to continue helping others. In the future, I plan to continue being a member of AMDREO, ensuring growth for myself and others.

Shaping Our Futures

Bella Ruan

During our weekly volunteer program, I have the opportunity to lead workshops designed to help students and neighbors in our community prioritize their mental health. These workshops emphasize personal growth, self-awareness, and a deeper understanding of one's own needs. As a workshop leader, it was my role to moderate the discussion, encourage participants to openly share their thoughts and ideas, and provide positive feedback on the different perspectives presented by the participants.

To create a safe and respectful environment, I ensured that each participant felt valued and protected when sharing their ideas. This included actively listening to each individual, recognizing the uniqueness of each person's perspective, and fostering a sense of inclusion and mutual respect among all participants.

By participating in these workshops, I have helped others and gained a great deal of knowledge that plays an important role in my daily life. These learning experiences have enabled me to be more effective in helping others, whether through providing guidance or simply being a supporter. The workshop was also transformative for me personally. I have become more confident, decisive, and willing to express my thoughts and opinions.

These changes have definitely enriched my life, making it more vibrant and fulfilling. Recognizing the impact that increased self-confidence has had on my own well-being, I now encourage my friends to embrace self-confidence, knowing that it will improve their lives as well. AMDREO volunteering has played a key role in my personal growth, allowing me to learn more about myself and feel confident in my abilities and aspirations. I have received a lot of positive feedback from my family, teachers and friends. They noticed a big change in my demeanor; I became more optimistic, outgoing, and clearer about my goals. This newfound clarity provided me with the tools to achieve my goals, allowing me to both capitalize on my strengths and receive support from those around me.

The workshops fostered a sense of community and camaraderie among the participants. Many people developed new friendships, and I developed a stronger connection to the participants and the content of the seminars. Each seminar reinforced the core messages of personal growth and mental health, making these volunteer activities a valuable part of my life.

AMDREO's volunteer activities have been extremely beneficial to me. Not only have they increased my self-confidence and self-awareness, but they have also strengthened my relationships and community connections. Workshops have taught us to value our mental health, understand our needs, and support each other's growth to be more colorful and connected.

I learned effective communication skills such as active listening and empathic engagement, which proved invaluable in both personal and academic settings. These skills have enabled me to build stronger, more meaningful relationships with those around me and to deal with conflict and challenges in a more relaxed and resilient manner. In addition, the sense of purpose and fulfillment I gained from helping others motivated me to explore more opportunities to get involved in my community. I began to participate in other volunteer activities and community projects, applying the principles of empathy, respect, and encouragement that I had developed in AMDREO. This broader involvement expanded my understanding of community dynamics and the various ways in which individuals contribute to the collective well-being.

As I look back on my journey with AMDREO, I am grateful for the growth and opportunities these programs have provided. Not only have they shaped me into a more confident and compassionate person, but they have also inspired me to continue advocating for mental health awareness and personal growth in all aspects of my life. The lasting impact of these experiences will undoubtedly continue to shape my future actions and ambitions.

My Gains in the Y.S.D.C. Seminar

Ariel Wang

My name is Ariel Wang. I am a first-year student at Crean Lutheran High School.

When I was in 10th grade, in order to improve my social practice and enrich my social experience, I participated in the "Y.E.T. Youth Growth Seminar" volunteer activity with my good friend Donald, and became a little leader six months later, every Sunday Based on the topics set in the "Youth Self-Growth" course, we led the students participating in the seminar to discuss and share their experiences and confusions in interpersonal communication.

Every Wednesday, I will organize a small team of leaders to make preliminary preparations for the Sunday evening seminar, such as designing ice-breaking games; selecting discussion topics for this issue; determining leaders and assistants, preparing supporting materials, etc. Because I am an independent child, I sometimes cannot listen to other people's opinions. Not only do I have a lot of quarrels with my parents, but I also have quarrels with my peers because of disagreements.

After receiving training on effective communication, I gradually understood the importance of communicating with people and the methods of effective communication. Especially in the process of leading YSDC, I tried to apply the knowledge I learned, tried to listen attentively, and made clear When expressing disagreements with peers, I also learned to control my bad emotions, listen to other people's suggestions, and effectively communicate and negotiate with everyone to reach a consensus. This process has allowed me to exercise and grow.

Since I became the junior leader of YSDC, my parents feel that I have made great progress, such as being more responsible and willing to help others. From February 2023 to May 2024, except when there are competitions or special events, I will attend seminars every Sunday without interruption. Hopefully, our discussion topics will help adults better understand teenagers' preferences, thoughts, and opinions. We also hope that through the seminar activities, teenagers can better communicate with their parents, grow up happily, and become the best versions of themselves.

A Journey to Foster Change and Growth

Bryan Wu

Ever since the discovery of the unconscious mind in the 20th century, humankind has finally begun to understand the concept of mental health. Following the footsteps of individuals digging deeper into the scientific field of psychology, the impact of society and family on an individual mentally has raised more and more attention. As we enter the 21st century, the concept of "mental health and awareness" has been given even more meaning; with social media becoming a new form of socializing and communication, mental issues in our community that were once dismissed and ignored are now finally being brought up. Particularly, these issues can have the biggest effects on the youth of our communities. Issues such as cyberbullying, identity struggle, and parental trauma are deeply woven into the fabric of the new generation. A big question mark remains for me on what changes I can bring to my community to contribute to building mental health awareness.

With this question in mind, I was introduced to AMDREO in 2023. I had the privilege of being a leader in a seminar hosted by this organization, focusing on youth mental development. Our seminar met weekly to discuss topics related to self-growth, communication skills, and fostering the growth of each member. Each session allowed me to contribute to our community while honing my leadership and interpersonal skills. As a seminar leader, I led and hosted discussions and organized activities, encouraging each seminar member to share their personal experience and opinions.

One of the most blissful experiences that serves as a testament to the impact of the seminar was seeing the growth of one of my peers. When he was first introduced to the seminar, he was fairly introverted and isolated from most of the discussions; I merely thought it would only take time before the group got to know and connect with him more. However, after my fellow seminar leaders reflected on this observation with his parents and discussed it, we realized that he was rejecting the idea of opening up to the rest of the group and speaking about his experience in front of others. To help him experience the seminar, I decided it would be a good idea to encourage him to be a part of hosting the weekly seminar so that he could feel the appreciation and welcome the group has for him. As he took on a leadership role, I observed that he gradually opened up to the rest of the group and was able to form connections with many of his peers. Witnessing this positive change was incredibly rewarding and reinforced the value of our volunteer efforts. This experience has also helped me grow personally. I initially struggled with letting him try on leadership roles, as I worried about the effect on the seminar. However, the results showed that being a leader is not always about taking on all the roles, nor is it about being the one that controls the order, but more so about letting people shine and reach their full potential.

Being a leader in the seminar has also made me realize my worth and what value I can hold. It has not only allowed me to give back to the community but also facilitated my personal growth in ways I hadn't anticipated. The skills and lessons learned will undoubtedly continue to benefit me in future endeavors.

The experience of volunteering at AMDREO has been rewarding and full of surprises. I am grateful to be part of the organization's effort to build mental health awareness. I am grateful to the founders, Mandy and Jeson Zhang, and the organization for providing such enriching opportunities.

Gaining Confidence in Social Situations

Sunny Chen

Throughout my year as a leader of the YSDC seminars, I taught various psychological topics related to improving socialization skills, self-control, and other topics related to personal growth to my peers. In the seminars, I encouraged sharing and discussion related to the topic of life experiences and ideas for personal growth. Based on my Seminar teaching experiences, I also introduced the Relationship Board Game. By playing this game, participants learn how to apply their youth development skills in a myriad of scenarios in a fun and entertaining manner. I enjoyed leading the seminar this year and had insightful discussions and ideas from my participants throughout the various topics we discussed.

In the seminar, if peers don't understand my topic, I can re-explain it and comprehensibly. For instance, when introducing the topic of effective communication with people to my peers, I narrowed my explanation down into clear, understandable words. Using colloquial language, my participants can better grasp the concept of the topic, engaging them in the discussion with interest. I also encouraged everyone to share their ideas with me so I could better understand their needs. With ideas shared by peers, I better understand the challenges they've gone through, and I can give them suggestions for improving their mental well-being.

Volunteer activities such as the weekly seminars and the Relationship Board Game helped me better understand the topics and apply various self-development skills such as active listening and self-control in everyday interactions. The seminar helped increase my confidence in understanding my own behavior and how I can control it to avoid conflict with others or myself from hearing about others' ideas and experiences. The relationship board game also helped me apply the knowledge I learned in the YSDC seminars and YET classes to real-life scenarios and understand how and when to apply it. The game was entertaining and kept me engaged and interested in learning about self-development skills for youth, and I enjoyed it very much.

Throughout my experience as a leader in the seminars, my teachers and friends helped me identify my strengths and weaknesses. For example, my parents also told me not to be authoritative or controlling others. I learned from my parents not to, for instance, confiscate participants' phones during the seminar, as their needs would not be met, and they would not feel content. Still, my teacher congratulated me on my diligence in guiding my participants through the seminar and helping them improve their self-development skills. My teacher also told me that I really helped others learn about the seminar topics and apply them in real life. Seeking feedback from family, teachers, and friends helped me identify my strengths and weaknesses to help me grow and become a likable leader.

I wanted to say a heartwarming thank you to Jeson Zhang and Mrs. Tang for helping me develop the youth efficiency skills to become a successful leader in the YSDC seminars. I learned effective communication skills between others and me to meet my needs without causing conflicts. I learned effective communication strategies from the YET classes, such as Method 3 for solving conflicts. Knowing how to apply the win-win method in conflicts helped me form better relationships with my family, teachers, and friends, as the method enabled everyone to get their needs met in a peaceful manner. Learning self-development skills like Method 3 can help me gain confidence in social interactions with others and is especially essential in leadership skills should any conflict occur and need to be solved in the seminar meetings.

Working Together to Succeed

YouYou Wang

If the heart is a tree. What kind of tree will you be? We are the unique cultivators of each tree. We come together to find ways to heal and grow each tree. As a cultivator who wants to be influential, I came to Youth Self-development. The little girl who used to have low self-esteem, be submissive, and dare not express herself has become a confident cultivator here. For every psychological problem, I no longer sit there like a doll, but actively raise my hands and bravely stand up as the first person to break the ice. As a practitioner of Wild Heart, I aspire to inspire others to embrace their uniqueness and cultivate their inner strength. I hope that I can be like a sunflower, showing my sunniest side to everyone and inspiring everyone. In every seminar, I actively arouse everyone's interest in this topic and create a lively and interesting environment. I am committed to giving everyone the right to share their experiences and stories, so that everyone can be a part of it, ask for help with questions, progress together, and grow together without fear of judgment. Of course, the mental health discussion that had the most profound impact on me was how to restrain and reasonably express one's negative emotions. Throughout this seminar, I deeply reflected on some of my conflicts with my family at home and my interactions with friends at school. I realized that whether I was socializing at home or outside, there would always be a lot of negative emotions. I made good use of the headline this time and told each cultivator about his or her own personal experience, such as the small conflicts at home due to conflicts with parents, and the estrangement caused by not wanting to accommodate friends at school. These are all triggers that can easily trigger negative emotions. In this regard, we all need to work hard to control our emotions. It's terrible not to be able to manage emotions kindly. It will cling to your tree like a pest until your tree collapses completely. But as a new generation of cultivators, we are not afraid of problems. If there are problems, we will actively look for solutions. This is why we are gathered here. In the face of these small contradictions, I proposed that we should be generous. These contradictions are the cracks in disagreements caused by everyone starting from different perspectives. All we have to do is close the crack and the tree can stand firm.

In this regard, we all need to work hard to control our emotions. It's terrible not to be able to manage emotions kindly. It will cling to your tree like a pest until your tree collapses completely. But as a new generation of cultivators, we are not afraid of problems. If there are problems, we will actively look for solutions. This is why we are gathered here. In the face of these small contradictions, I proposed that we should be generous. These contradictions are the cracks in disagreements caused by everyone starting from different perspectives. All we have to do is close the crack and the tree can stand firm. We can reasonably arrange our leisure time to do some extracurricular sports to give the tree enough oxygen and sunlight. We can also read books quietly and listen to music to make the tree feel comfortable. You can also express your thoughts directly, take the initiative to confess your views to family and friends, and resolve misunderstandings and conflicts. These are all good ways to deal with emotions. In this regard, we all need to work hard to control our emotions. It's terrible not to be able to manage emotions kindly. It will cling to your tree like a pest until your tree collapses completely. But as a new generation of cultivators, we are not afraid of problems. If there are problems, we will actively look for solutions. This is why we are gathered here. In the face of these small contradictions, I proposed that we should be generous. These contradictions are the cracks in disagreements caused by everyone starting from different perspectives. All we have to do is close the crack and the tree can stand firm. We can reasonably arrange our leisure time to do some extracurricular sports to give the tree enough oxygen and sunlight. We can also read books quietly and listen to music to make the tree feel enough comfort. You can also express your thoughts directly, take the initiative to confess your views to family and friends, and resolve misunderstandings and conflicts. These are all good ways to deal with emotions. Look, in fact, it is not that difficult to deal with emotions. As long as you cultivate it carefully, the tree will grow up healthily. This is just a small part of this lecture, and it is each small part that brings together our entire youth mental health growth club. It is through the youth mental health growth community that we have the opportunity to share experiences, support each other and learn effective coping strategies. We can build a healthier and stronger mental state so that everyone can grow up on the road to success. Find support and encouragement. It is this kind of joint efforts and solidarity that makes us a vibrant and hopeful society, contributing to the growth of young people's mental health.

Chapter 4: Accompanying Children's Growth as My Own

The YSDC seminar leaders are trained volunteers, along with their parents. The weekly seminars are possible due to the efforts of both the leaders and parents. This is a compilation of the thoughts of a few parents. Let us see that accompanying the growth of children is the best opportunity for parents to grow themselves.

带领青少年自我成长研讨会的领袖们都是经过培训的青少年义工，他们的父母也都是这个活动的志愿者。每期的研讨会都是这些青少年义工领袖和父母志愿者们共同努力的成果。这个章节收录了一些志愿者父母们的心声，让我们看到陪伴孩子的成长，正是父母们自我成长的最佳契机。

成长之路，就是学会爱

Wendy Cao

2022 年用一念天堂一念地狱来形容我和女儿的关系再贴切不过。曾经我还挺沾沾自喜自己的教育方式呢，可就在女儿进入六年级快十一岁时我真的笑不起来了，我的教育方式基本失效了，女儿对我说的最多说的就是 No，我们娘俩的战争动不动就会爆发。渐渐地她宁可在虚拟世界里倾注和投入精力和情感也不愿和我多说一句话。更让我抓狂的是一个月三、四次不交作业，学习成绩一落千丈。我软硬兼施，恩威并济，可是效果却是我们的关系越来越紧张，只要谈到有关学习和使用电子产品的问题就是剑拔弩张的。我每天都在焦虑中度过，女儿也常常感觉我不理解她，她感觉很孤独、更觉得自己很糟糕。我意识到问题已经到了非常严重的程度了，每天都在想该怎么解决这个难题？但是结果总是事与愿违。

当我一筹莫展的时候朋友带我走进了漫谈心和 P.E.T.父母效能训练的课堂，当我第一次听到 Mandy 老师的亲子关系的公开课，就深深的被吸引了，我感觉到了希望。没有任何犹豫地就报名了第二十期父母效能训练的课程，我明白了倾听的重要性，课堂上练习沟通技巧，清晰人际关系中关系优先，深刻的理解同理心与无条件接纳。

我开始一点点地把我所学的用在和女儿的相处上，虽然一开始我时不时的还会发沟通绊脚石，但是因为有意识就可以及时止损。渐渐地就这么无声无息地产生作用了，记得有一次女儿因太累了不想去上小提琴课，以前的我一定会因为担心轻易妥协会让她遇到困难就退缩，进而会使用权威让她坚持，不免又是一次冲突。可我试着同理和倾听孩子，我想母女关系比起一节课更重要，所以也说出了自己的担心可是因为理解女儿确实太累上课效果也不会好，就帮她请了假。当时女儿的眼神里充满了光，拥抱着对我说："谢谢妈妈的理解！" 要知道有一段时间我们母女都没有亲密的肢体接触了。（神奇的是并没有因为我的妥协女儿会"躺平"，她休息了大约半小时后主动练习了一小时小提琴，而且也很认真的完成了功课。）这件事对我感触至深，当父母能够接纳和理解孩子时孩子呈现出来的是超出我们的预期。

暑期女儿参加了漫谈心第二期 Y.E.T.青少年效能训练的课程，她从中学会了如何面对青春期的困惑和人际关系的处理，她也被身为助教的 Jeson 所感染。原本害羞的女儿也能大方的站在台前分享感悟。我在 P.E.T 的环境中几期复训浸泡，越来越明白不给孩子贴标签、沟通时用我信息表达、懂得双方的需求都很重要、用第三法解决冲突等等有多重要。

转眼已经来到了 2024 年，我女儿加入了 Jeson 发起的青少年自我成长俱乐部，渐渐成长为 Yorba Linda 城市组的青少年义工领袖，我也因为深深受益而义不容辞的承担起了父母志愿者主席的职位，我和女儿一起做公益活动，希望影响更多人来做公益，来自我成长活出幸福。

俱乐部已经运营了第三个年头了，女儿越发的自信与自律，我们的亲子关系越发的融洽。当女儿被问到：如果你遇到困境或者情绪低落的时你能想到的最温暖和接纳你的人是谁？她毫不犹豫地回答：我的妈妈。我是百感交集啊！

现在的女儿常常跟我分享她在学校里、和同学们、朋友们的一些有趣的、烦恼的、困惑的事情，我们重新建立了信任和亲密关系。我再也不用像一个"间谍"一样盯着女儿使用电子产品的时间和监督她的学习了，我们自由的聊开心的不开心的事情，一起出门旅行。尽管也有一些反复和周折，但是我最终选择用爱、信任和耐心陪伴女儿成长。这一切都归于有 P.E.T.和 Y.E.T.的环境、有漫谈心这个大团队的支持。

记得 Mandy 老师在课堂上经常说的一句话："只要父母肯做一点改变，就能把孩子向上向善的能力激发出来"。现在女儿活跃在漫谈心青少年的各种活动中，那个自信、阳光、快乐的女儿又回到我的身边了，孩子的内驱力和责任心也在慢慢建立。自我成长的过程的同时在帮助更多的小伙伴，收益颇丰！

我和女儿的自我成长之路，作为漫谈心人最深的体会就是漫谈心让我们学会了如何沟通如何去爱！

从鸡飞狗跳到母慈子笑

Madison An

我是 Jeson Zhang 发起的漫谈心青少年自我成长俱乐部
Y.S.D.C.的眾多父母志愿者中的一员，很久之前我就想寫一
些東西來表達對漫談心的感激之情，只是一直沒有抽出時
間，現在終於可以難靜下心來寫一寫自己的内心所想。當我
閉上眼睛回想著自己自從成為母親跌跌撞撞一路走來，心中
五味雜陳。之前一直天真地以為越努力越幸運，現在才突然
意識到原來曾經自己一直在錯誤的方向一路狂奔，如果方法
是錯的，再努力也徒勞，還好有漫談心，讓我的育兒之路不
再艱辛。

1. 青春期帶來的煩惱

我來自天津，有兩個可愛的孩子，大女兒 Melody
Deng 15 歲了，回想起自從女兒的出生到點滴成長，10 歲
之前可以肯定的說，是欣喜自豪與感動，但過了 10 歲不知
從哪天開始腦海中浮現的大多都是衝突對抗甚至難飛狗跳。
正如大多數家庭所經歷的一樣，女兒的青春期讓家庭由晴轉
陰，前一秒或許還晴空萬里，後一秒就雷雨交加......我迷茫
了，感到了一種前所未有的力不從心，我開始思考這一切是
如何發生的並尋找解決方法。

2. 為什麼物質豐富的 21 世紀, 孩子們的青春期變得如此顯化?

從價值觀來說, 20 世紀的父母認為把書讀好是最重要的, 讀書才是翻身的機會, 但 21 世紀的孩子會認為只要有小確幸, 能快快樂樂的上網, 就是人生的幸福。

從心理特質來說, 20 世紀的父母長期面對生存壓力, 是理性和務實的, 在情感面是壓抑的。而 21 世紀的孩子因為沒有像父母一樣經歷人生挑戰, 不能理解父母為什麼這麼看重學習, 於是有強烈的情緒衝突, 導致在認知發展方面的錯位。

3. 以上的差異造成許多家庭間親子關係的衝突甚至傷害。然而更困難的是, 當父母認識到這點, 想要改善親子關係的時候, 卻發現有「想做卻做不到的問題」。例如: 自己都有很多情緒困擾, 如何能心平氣和的面對孩子的各種問題? 自己從小到大所接受的權威主義, 已經很難改變。面對與孩子想法的差異, 除了使用父母權柄, 還有其他方法讓孩子聽話嗎?

4. 學習 P.E.T.和 Y.E.T., 使用了正確的溝通方式, 親子關係得到極大改善。

來到美國後, 經過好朋友 Wendy 的推薦, 我和女兒有幸參加了 Manndy 老師帶領的 "P.E.T.父母效能训练" 工作坊，我女儿也参加了 Jeson 做助教的.YE.T.青少年效能训练的課程，從此我和女兒的關係悄悄發生了改變。

我之前總是抱怨孩子為什麼這麼不懂事，不知道體諒父母的辛苦呢？通過學習戈登博士的課程，才意識到首先需要改變的是父母，而不是孩子！孩子都是天使，他們雖然身體已經發育，看上去高高大大，但思想尚未成熟，不能让孩子成为家庭的拯救者；相反幸福的家庭才能成就孩子。

我之前的溝通方式太過簡單粗暴，由於自己已經習慣於從自我感受出發，使用的都是你信息和絆腳石，讓孩子接受到都是負面的，發生問題意見不一致的時候也只是使用父母權威，要求孩子無條件服從，久而久之這種錯誤的方式在孩子青春期到來的時候會顯露出它的弊端。

現在通過學習 P.E.T.課程，我懂得了黨孩子有負面情緒的時候，需要一個聆聽者和支持者，而非說教。我和女兒也懂得了如何有效溝通，遇到問題使用積極傾聽和第三法，盡量尋求讓每一方都滿意的方式。漸漸的女儿也从"刺猬"逐漸柔和下来，善良而又自律，情商越来越高。過程中雖然有時也會一不小心使用之前錯誤的方式，但至少自己心裡馬上能意識到，只是仍然需要時間來慢慢練習。現在女兒已經在青少年自我成长俱乐部 Y.S.D.C.成為了一名合格的 Leader（领袖），相信良好的溝通方式會内化為良好的品格而伴隨她一生，實現自己的理想，成為自己想要的樣子。

最後我想說的是：感謝漫談心為廣大華人家庭帶來福音，感恩自己如此幸運！

积极沟通、共同成长

Sissi Chen

对于大多数移民美国的华裔家庭，特别是像我们这样父母英文不好的家庭，我相信大家都面对同样的难题，那就是和青春期的子女有不可逾越的代沟，这包括了年龄的代沟，以及更严重的文化代沟。

很感谢 Mandy 老师带领的 P.E.T.父母效能训练和 Jeson 助教的 Y.E.T.青少年效能训练课程，让我和孩子一起学习有效沟通。特别是 Jeson 在此基础上成立的"Y.S.D.C.青少年自我成长义工俱乐部"，不仅使我们在课堂上学到的知识可以实际应用，更是给了家长和孩子一个共同成长的平台。

起初女儿 Ariel 想成为研讨会小领袖的时候，她有一些担忧和犹豫，怕自己不能胜任。我鼓励她勇于突破自己。如果是从前，我的作用可能就停留在这个层面上了。但在学习了戈登博士的父母效能训练后，我明白倾听才是更好的沟通渠道，要明白孩子行为话语深层的需求，才能更好的支持她。于是我和女儿就要不要担任小领袖进行了一次深入的谈话。这次谈话使我真正了解到她的需求，女儿希望我也能承担志愿家长的工作，这样她会更有勇气，会更了解他们的义工研讨会在做什么，可以在她需要的时候，给予有效的帮助。

当了解到女儿的实际需求后，其实我也面临了很大的挑战，对于来美后就一直在家做主妇的我，能不能做好志愿家长，能不能和大家团结合作，能不能坚持对是我要面考虑的问题。这时候才发现，原来一句简单的"我支持你"。没有什么实质作用，对孩子真正的支持是陪伴，是与他/她共同面对困难，一起承担责任。于是我也踏出了我的舒适圈，成为了尔湾森林湖城市组的家长负责人。

在共同带领义工研讨会的过程中，我和女儿确实遇到了很多问题，不同的意见，比如如何使研讨会的形式更活泼，更能吸引人；在活动期间对于电子设备的使用；课后作业谁来监督等等。每到这个时候，我们就尝试用有效地沟通——第三法来解决。虽然过程也会产生分歧或争辩，但慢慢地我们总会达成共识。而这样的沟通也逐渐渗透到生活中，是我和女儿不再像以前争吵不断，最后不得不用大人的身份来压制她。看到女儿的成长，更看到自己的成长，真的很欣慰。

孩子更自信，母子更亲密

Yan Wang

当我得知有戈登博士的青少年成长项目时，我怀着满心期待与信心让我家高中男孩加入了美国漫谈心理 Jeson zhang 组织的 Y.S.D.C.的青少年成长研讨会，我家孩子正处于青春发育期，他性格较羞涩，在学校里也不是社交能人，平时也在同学面前也不善于表达与沟通，我觉得他非常适合参加这个项目，相信能帮助他勇于表达自己的想法，在学校里能交到真正的朋友，遇到问题能找到解决问题的方法。通过参加了半年多的学习与尝试，孩子告诉我他非常喜欢成长研讨会，他觉得可以从每位同学那里感同身受地了解到他们在学校的社交、情绪控制及与父母有效沟通的问题等等，并促使他去学习并思考这些问题，从而让自己将来能有效地改善自己。

通过这段时间的学习，孩子越来越喜欢青少年成长这个主题，并对青少年健康成长心理学产生了较大兴趣，他主动提出了参加青少年成长 leader 培训项目：Mandy 老师带领 Jeson 助教的戈登博士的 "Y.E.T.青少年效能训练工作坊"。通过为期四周的实际操作学习，他专注于如何挖掘了解自己的内在需求，如何有效与他人沟通并表达，主动倾听，如何解决与他人在相处中出现的问题。同时这些方法也适用于与父母的沟通相处中，我也参加了漫谈心的 "P.E.T.父母效能训练工作坊"。

有一天孩子兴奋地告诉我他在学校交友时应用了 "积极倾听" 特别是当同学需要他的情感支持时倾听他们， 主动表达自己的感受和想法， 积极参与同学的谈话，他感觉喜欢他的同学越来越多了，他一下就变得有自信了。而当他主动表达自己的需求时运用 "我信息"，他发现同学们也更理解和接受他了，而不是像以前那样遇到不喜欢的事情只知道说 "不"。 他觉得学到的方法真的可以帮助他解决问题，有时与同学发生观念冲突时他也能运用学到的 "第三法" 找到问题的根本，运用排除与补充解决法去找到解决问题的最佳方法从而避免与同学产生矛盾。

目前孩子在学校的社交取得了较大进步， 他能理解同学们的行为与表达，也能准确地表达自己内心的真正需求，去交到更多的朋友。现在在家里也认真倾听我的需求然后表达出他自己的想法及需要，当我们的双方需求不能达成一致时，找出解决问题的方法，避免了我们之间的矛盾及冲突产生。现在孩子成为了成长研讨会的 leader（领袖），每次他都自信满满地与同学研讨每个主题，同学们的反馈都不错。

我能看到孩子在这个项目学习中全面成长了，他在学校交朋友也越来越顺利，每天的心情也越来越好，与父母能有效沟通，减少了正面冲突，我们之间也越来越亲密了。

当我看到孩子这些真实的改变，心理感慨万千，我们作为父母总说要多关爱孩子，但殊不知原来我们常常以爱的名义在绑架孩子，总是趾高气扬的站在父母的至高点去要求他们太多，似乎好像除了关注他们的学习，其它的都不重要，殊不知孩子在青春期的健康成长与心理发育才是最影响他一辈子幸福的关键问题。

所以我感恩漫谈心的针对父母和青少年自我成长俱乐部中针对孩子的一系列教育项目，让我们和孩子都在成熟在不断的发现与完善自己。

鼓励与回馈

Lucy Liu

Bryan 从 2022 年底开始对心灵成长、心理课程产生兴趣后，在 Mandy 老师和 Jeson Zhang 助教的 Y.E.T.青少年效能训练课程，逐渐学习了人本主义理念的青少年成长沟通课程，并且在 2023 年加入了 Jeson 发起的青少年自我成长俱乐部 Y.S.D.C.的公益研讨会项目，现在已经成长成为一名义工领袖。

Bryan 每周坚持积极为 club 的青少年研讨活动进行投入，参与并带动研讨课题的讨论，每次活动为团队提供前后场地组织清洁、配套服务，支持俱乐部的课题推进、深入与完成。作为一名积极的义工与 Leader，为漫谈心公益组织的研讨活动、形成项目研究报告、带动青少年及父母沟通、推动青少年成长的工作中付出了辛勤的义工劳动。

我看到 Bryan 在俱乐部中的点点滴滴的进步，他的认真和负责的态度，在团队领导及人际沟通，以及学术方面的积累，作为家长，我非常为他骄傲

同时，获得 2023 年度的总统义工奖是一个鼓励，我也希望 Bryan 继续坚持，以公益和向善的美德，继续在自己感兴趣的公益领域，积极服务与回赠周边人群、服务我们的社会！

<u>References</u>

https://www.pinterest.com/pin/47449651071636
2146/

https://www.threads.net/@appleeye191919/post/
C-2x4VGSpxK

https://www.gordontraining.com/

Parent Effectiveness Training by Dr. Thomas Gordon

Leader Effectiveness Training by Dr. Thomas Gordon

Teacher Effectiveness Training by Dr. Thomas Gordon

Sales Effectiveness Training by Dr. Thomas Gordon and Carl D. Zaiss

Youth Effectiveness Training Skillbook by Linda Adams

Be Your Best by Linda Adams

Made in the USA
Las Vegas, NV
03 December 2024

13228615R10069